Dreamcatcher Tutorials

Crochet Dream Catcher Patterns for Beginners

Copyright © 2021

All rights reserved.

DEDICATION

The author and publisher have provided this e-book to you for your personal use only. You may not make this e-book publicly available in any way. Copyright infringement is against the law. If you believe the copy of this e-book you are reading infringes on the author's copyright, please notify the publisher at: https://us.macmillan.com/piracy

Contents

Easy Crochet Dream Catcher 1

Lotus Flower Dream Catcher 6

Black Dream Catcher 16

Pineapple Snowflake Suncatcher 21

Tunisian Feathers 25

Crocheted 31

Spiral Dream Catcher 47

Dreamcatcher With Mille Colori 54

Brown Spiral Dream Catcher 58

Easy Crochet Dream Catcher

What you need

Embroidery hoop 10 cm diameter

Worsted weight yarn (I used white)

4.00 mm & 4.5 mm (G/6 & 7 hook)

Tapestry needle

White thread

Decorative items (beads, fabric scraps, ribbon, lace, cords, yarn)

Instructions

Hoop

First take aside your hoop; we will be needing only the inner hoop. Using white yarn and 4.5mm (US. 7) hook, sc around the hoop, ss, to the first sc, to join. Ch 60 and ss, to joining st, to create the hanger. Fasten off.

Doily

Using white and 4.00 mm hook (US G/6) Start with a magic ring or ch 4 and ss, to first ch to form a ring. Rnd 1: Ch 3 (counts as first dc), 11 dc into magic loop/ or ch 4 ring. Slip into 3rd chain of beginning ch 3. (12 sts).

Rnd 2: Ch 5 (counts as dc, ch 2). (Dc, ch 2) in each stitch around. Slip into 3rd chain of beginning ch 5. (12 dc and 12 loops)

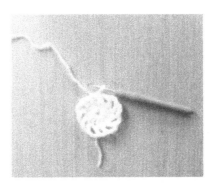

Rnd 3: Slip into ch 2 space. *(Dc, ch 2) twice into ch 2 space. Dc, ch 2 in next ch 2 space. Repeat from * around. Slip into first dc. Bind off. (18 dc and 18 loops)

Rnd 4: Sl st in ch-1 sp, ch 1, sc in same sp, ch 6, [sc in next ch-1 sp, ch 6] around; join with sl st to first sc. (18 sc and 18 ch-6 sps)

Rnd 5: Sl st in ch-1 sp, ch 1, sc in same sp, ch 7, [sc in next ch-1 sp, ch 7] around; join with sl st to first sc. (18 sc and 18 ch-6 sps)

Fasten off.

If your hoop is smaller just work fewer Rounds. If it is larger repeat Round 5, but increase the number of working chains in each Round. For example Round 6 would be: [sc in next ch-1 sp, ch 8] around.

Assembly:

Using your tapestry needle sew the doily on the hoop. Alternatively use some white thread and tie the edges of the doily to the hoop with thread.

Make up:

Gather all your decorative items, lace ribbon etc. and start tying to the bottom of your dreamcatcher. Using yarn make a long chain and tie to the bottom of your dreamcatcher. If desired add beads, or feathers.

That's it!

Lotus Flower Dream Catcher

What you need

Yarn:

DMC Natura Just Cotton in the following colours. I crocheted each round in order of colour.

Col A – Amaranto

Col B – Spring Rose

Col C – Acanthe

Col D – Ble

Col E – Light Green

Col F – Jade

Col G – Aquamarine

Col H – Bleu Layette

Col I – Blue Jeans

Hook: Size 3.5mm was used but I would recommend a 3.25mm to have the crocheted piece stretch more when attached onto the ring.

Ring: 250mm ring (I used a Shamrock Craft Plastic Beige 250mm ring from Spotlight)

Yarn needle

Scissors

Ribbon or lace of your choice

Stitches and Abbreviations used:

Chain (ch)

Single Crochet (sc): Starting with a loop on your hook, insert hook in stitch or space indicated and draw up a loop (two loops on hook). Yarn over and pull through both loops on your hook.

Standing Single Crochet: Starting with a slip stitch on your hook, insert hook in stitch or space indicated and draw up a loop (two loops on hook). Yarn over and pull through both loops on your hook.

Half Double Crochet (hdc): Starting with a loop on your hook, yarn over, insert hook in stitch or space indicated, yarn over and draw up a loop (three loops on hook. Yarn over and pull through all three loops.

Double Crochet (dc): Starting with a loop on your hook, yarn over, insert hook in stitch or space indicated, yarn over and draw up a loop (three loops on hook). Yarn over and pull through two loops (two loops on hook). Yarn over and pull through both loops on your hook.

Standing Double Crochet: Starting with a slip stitch on your hook, yarn over, insert hook in stitch or space indicated, yarn over and draw up a loop (three loops on hook). Yarn over and pull through two loops (two loops on hook). Yarn over and pull through both loops on your hook.

Treble Crochet (tr): Starting with a loop on your hook, yarn over twice, insert hook in stitch or space indicated, yarn over and draw up a loop (4 loops on hook). (Yarn over and pull through two loops) x

3 times

Cluster 2 (cl2): Starting with a loop on your hook, *yarn over, insert hook in stitch or space indicated, yarn over and draw up a loop (3 loops on hook), yarn over and pull through two loops*, repeat from * once, yarn over and pull through all (4) loops.

Cluster 3 (cl3): Starting with a loop on your hook, *yarn over, insert hook in stitch or space indicated, yarn over and draw up a loop (3 loops on hook), yarn over and pull through two loops*, repeat from * two times, yarn over and pull through all loops.

Standing cl2: Starting with a slip stitch on your hook, *yarn over, insert hook in stitch or space indicated, yarn over and draw up a loop (3 loops on hook), yarn over and pull through two loops*, repeat from * twice, yarn over and pull through all loops.

V stitch (v st): dc, ch 3, dc in same sp

V treble stitch (v-tr): tr, ch 3, tr in same sp

Join with slip stitch (jss)

Instructions

Round 1:

Using Col A; in a magic ring, ch 3 (counts as dc), 15 dc in ring, jss to top of ch 3 made.

(16 dc)

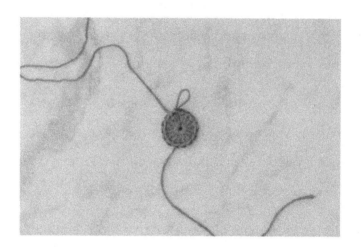

Round 2:

Using Col A; Ch 4 (counts as dc + ch), (dc + ch 1) in each st around, jss to 3rd ch made. Cut yarn and fasten off.

(16 dc, 16 x ch-1 sp)

Round 3:

Using Col B; In any ch-1 sp, make a standing cl2, ch 5, (cl2, ch 5) in each ch-1 sp around, jss to 1st cl2 made. Cut yarn and fasten off.

(16 cl2, 16 x ch-5 sp)

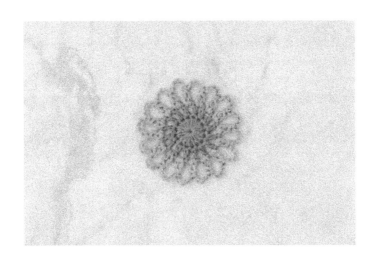

Round 4:

Using Col C; In any ch-5 sp, make a standing sc, ch 7, (sc, ch 7) in each ch-5 sp around, jss to 1st sc made. Cut yarn and fasten off.

(16 sc, 16 x ch-7 sp)

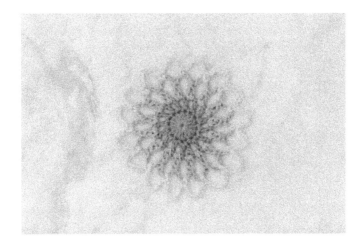

Round 5:

Using Col D; In any ch-7 sp, make a standing sc, ch 9, (sc, ch 9) in each ch-7 sp around, jss to 1st sc made. Cut yarn and fasten off.

(16 dc, 16 x ch-9 sp)

Round 6:

Using Col E; In any ch-9 sp, make a standing dc, 4 dc in same sp, ch 3, (5 dc, ch 3) in each ch-9 sp around, jss to 1st sc made. Cut yarn and fasten off.

(16 x 5 dc groups, 16 x ch-3 sp)

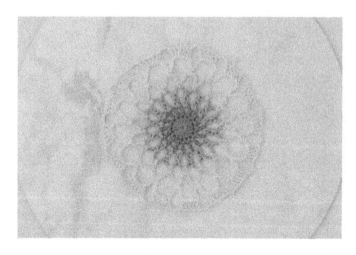

Round 7:

Using Col F; In any ch-3 sp, make a standing dc, (ch 3, dc) in same sp, ch 2, skip 2 dc, sc in next dc (middle dc of 5 dc group), ch 2, skip 2 dc, *v st in next ch-3 sp, ch 2, skip 2 dc, sc in next dc, ch 2, skip 2 dc*, repeat from * around, jss to 1st dc. Cut yarn and fasten off.

(16 x v st, 16 sc, 32 x ch-2 sp)

Round 8:

Using Col G; In any ch-3 sp from v st from round 7, make a standing cl3, ch 3, cl3 in same sp, ch 2, skip 2 ch sts, sc in sc from round 7, ch 2, skip 2 ch sts, *(cl3, ch 3, cl3) in next ch-3 sp, ch 2, skip 2 ch sts, sc in sc, ch 2, skip 2 ch sts*, repeat from * around, jss to top of 1st cl3 made. Cut yarn and fasten off.

(16 x [cl3, ch 3, cl3], 16 x sc, 32 x ch-2 sp)

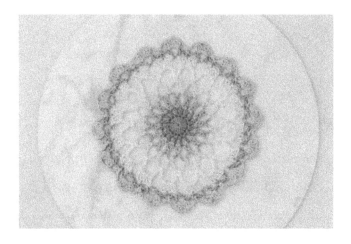

Round 9:

Using Col H; In any ch-3 sp made in round 8, make a standing dc, (ch 3, dc) in same sp, ch 1, skip 3 sts (cl3, 2 ch), v-tr in sc made in round 8, ch 1, skip 3 st (2 ch, cl3), *v st in ch-3 sp, ch 1, skip 3 sts, v-tr in sc, ch 1, skip 3 sts* repeat from * around, jss to 1st v st. Cut yarn and fasten off.

(16 x v st, 16 x v-tr, 16 x sc, 32 x ch-1 sp)

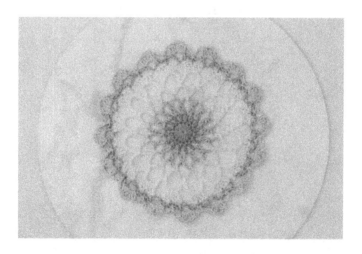

Round 10:

Using Col I; In any ch-3 sp (it doesn't matter if it's from the v st or v-tr st), make a standing sc, (sc, ch 1 2 sc) in same sp, skip st, sc in ch-1 sp, skip st, (2 sc, ch 1, 2 sc) in ch-3 sp, skip st, sc in ch-1 sp*, repeat from * around, jss to 1st sc made. Cut yarn and weave in ends.

(160 sc, 32 x ch-1)

Dreamcatcher Tutorials

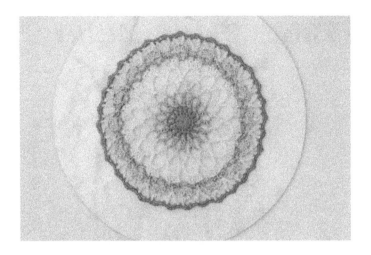

To attach to hoop, cut a piece of yarn the same material that you just used about 1m/40 inches. Thread onto needle, insert needle through ch-1 sp of any 'point' made in the last round, holding the crocheted part inside the hoop, thread needle under hoop, bringing it back over the top and into the next ch -1 sp, repeat around and fasten off, weave in yarn.

To get the same look as this new dream catcher, repeat this, but go the other way so you criss-cross over the ones already made.

Cut ribbon/lace into desired length and attach to bottom oh hoop using a slip knot method. I think it's called something like that, Fold ribbon in half and insert the middle (loop part) through the sp created when attaching crocheted part to hoop, pull wrap over the 'legs' of the ribbon.

Black Dream Catcher

What you need

I used Patons 4ply Cotton in Black

3.25mm recommended hook

Scissors

Dreamcatcher Tutorials

Yarn needle

10 inch / 25.5cm hoop (bought this one from Lincraft for the Aussies)

– Ribbon or lace for detail

Notes:

– This pattern is written in US terms

– Not as hard as you think

Stitches and Abbreviations Used:

– sc = single crochet

– ch = chain

– ch sp = chain sp

– dc = double crochet

– dc2tog = double crochet 2 together

-dc3tog = double crochet 3 together

– tr = treble

-sl st = slip stich

Dreamcatcher Tutorials

Instructions

1: Make magic ring, ch3, 15dc in ring, join with sl st (16sts)

2: ch4 counts as dc + ch1, (dc + ch1) in each st around join with sl st (16sts)

3: sl st to ch sp, (ch2 counts as start of dc2tog), dc in same sp, ch5, (dc2tog + ch5) in each ch sp around, join with sl st to first dc2tog (16 loops)

4: sl st in first 2 sts of ch5, sc into ch sp, ch7, *(sc in next sp + ch7)* repeat around, join with sl st to first sc (16 loops)

5: sl st in first 3 sts of ch7, sc into ch sp, ch 9, *(sc in next sp + ch9)* repeat around, join with sl st to first sc (16 loops)

6: sl st in first 4 sts of ch9, (ch 3, 3dc) in same sp, ch3, (5dc + ch3) in each sp around, make dc in the first loop (beginning ch-9 sp you worked in), (16x 5dcs)

7: sl st in next to sts so that you are in the middle dc from previous round, ch3 counts as sc + ch 2, *(dc, ch3, dc) in next sp, ch 2, sc in middle dc from previous round, ch 2* repeat around 14 more times, (dc, ch3, dc) in next sp, ch 2, join to first sc with sl st.

8: ch3 (counts as sc + ch2), *(dc3tog, ch2, dc3tog) in next ch3 sp, ch

2, sc into sc from previous round, ch2*, repeat around 14 more times, (dc3tog, ch 3, dc3tog) in next sp, ch2, join with sl st to 1st ch of ch3 at the beginning of the round.

9: ch7 (counts as tr + ch3), tr in same st, ch1, *(dc, ch3, dc) in sp between dc3togs from previous round, ch1, (tr, ch3, tr) into sc from previous round, ch1* repeat around 14 more times, (dc, ch3, dc) in next sp between dc3tog, ch1, join with sl st to the 4th ch.

10: *(2sc, ch2, 2sc) in ch3 sp, sc in next ch1 sp*, repeat around and join with sl st to first sc. Cut, secure yarn and weave in end.

To attach to hoop, cut a piece of yarn the same material that you just used about 1m/40 inches. Thread onto needle, insert needle through ch2 sp of any 'point' made in the last round, holding the crocheted part inside the hoop, thread needle under hoop, bringing it back over the top and into the next ch2 sp, repeat around and fasten off, weave in yarn.

Cut ribbon/lace into desired length and attach to bottom oh hoop using a slip knot method. I think it's called something like that, Fold ribbon in half and insert the middle (loop part) through the sp created when attaching crocheted part to hoop, pull wrap over the 'legs' of the ribbon, they just look like hanging legs to me lol, so that it creates a loop. Kind of like when you attach tassels to blankets, my brain has gone blank, I am not even sure if you call them tassels now lol. Sleep deprivation will do that to you.

Pineapple Snowflake Suncatcher

What you need

Size 10 Crochet Thread (Knit-Cro-Sheen): White – 75 yards; Brass Ring – 11" round; Large Sewing Needle; ¼" wide Satin Ribbon – Peach, 8" long; Ribbon Rose – Peach; Hot Glue.

Note: Since Cotton stretches over time it's a good idea to make sure your piece is a tight fit when sewing it onto the ring. You may want to increase the ring size for a tighter fit depending on the size of your piece.

Crochet Hook: Steel size 7 (1.65 mm) or size needed to obtain gauge.

Gauge: Rnd 1 = 1¾"

Special Stitches

Cluster Stitch (cl-st): Keeping last lp of each st on hook, work 3 tr or 5 tr in st or sp indicated, yo and draw through all lps on hook.

SUNCATCHER

Rnd 1: (Right Side) Starting at center, ch 6, join with sl st to first ch to form ring; ch 4, keeping last lp of ea st on hook work 4 tr in ring, yo, draw through all lps on hook (beg cluster made), ch 7, (5 tr cl-st in ring, ch 7) 5 times; join with sl st to top of beg cl-st. (6 cl-sts)

DO NOT TURN EACH ROUND.

Rnd 2: Ch 1, (sc, hdc, 7dc, hdc, sc) in next ch-7 sp around; join with sl st to first sc. (6 Shells)

Rnd 3: Ch 8 (counts as first dc and ch 5), dc in same st as joining, ch 5, sc in center dc of next shell, * ch 5, (dc, ch 5, dc) in sp between next 2 shells, ch 5, sc in center dc of next shell; rep from * around; ending with ch 2, dc in first dc (this join brings thread in position for next Rnd). (12 dc, 6 sc)

Rnd 4: Ch 1, sc in same sp as joining, ch 3, (dc, ch 1) 7 times in next ch-5 sp, ch 2, sc in next ch-5 sp, * ch 5, sc in next ch-5 sp, ch 3, (dc, ch 1) 7 times in next ch-5 sp, ch 2, sc in next ch-5 sp; rep from * around, ending with ch 2, dc to first sc. (42 dc, 12 sc)

Rnd 5: Ch 1, sc in same sp as joining, ch 3, (3 tr cl-st in next ch-1 sp, ch 1) 3 times, ch 2, (3 tr cl-st in next ch-1 sp, ch 1) 3 times, ch 2, * sc in next ch-5 sp, ch 3, (3 tr cl-st in next ch-1 sp, ch 1) 3 times, ch 2, (3 tr cl-st in next ch-1 sp, ch 1) 3 times, ch 2, rep from * around, join with sl st to first sc. (36 Clusters)

Rnd 6: Ch 9 (counts as first tr and ch 5), ** (3 tr cl-st in next ch-1 sp, ch 2) twice, (3 tr cl-st, ch 5, 3 tr cl-st) in ch-3 sp, (ch 2, 3 tr cl-st in next ch-1 sp) twice,** ch 5, * tr in next sc, ch 5, (3 tr cl-st in next ch-1 sp, ch 2) twice, (3 tr cl-st, ch 5, 3 tr cl-st) in ch-3 sp, (ch 2, 3 tr cl-st in ch-1 sp) twice, ch 5, rep from * around, join with sl st to first tr. (36 Clusters)

Rnd 7: Ch 9 (counts as first tr and ch 5), tr in same ch as joining, ch 3, (3 tr cl-st in next ch-1 sp, ch 2) twice, (3 tr cl-st, ch 5, 3 tr cl-st) in ch-3 sp, (ch 2, 3 tr cl-st in next ch-1 sp) twice, ch 3, * (tr, ch 5, tr) in next tr, ch 3, (3 tr cl-st in next ch-1 sp, ch 2) twice, (3 tr cl-st, ch 5, 3 tr cl-st) in ch-3 sp, (ch 2, 3 tr cl-st in next ch-1 sp) twice, ch 3, rep from * around, join with sl st to first tr. Finish off and weave in ends.

Finishing

– Using Needle and Crochet Thread, stretch and sew points to Brass ring.

– Tie a 2½" Bow and glue to center of Suncatcher.

– Glue Rose over center of Bow.

Tunisian Feathers

What you need

5mm crochet hook without handle (pop a rubber band on the end to keep your stitches from falling off)

DK/8ply cotton in at least 2 colours

Instructions

Large Feather

Pattern notes:

The following instructions are for the design pictured above (the little guy sitting out on his own) but you can go to town with as many colours as you like (or could be bothered weaving in the ends of), mix up the stripe sequence as you please. There are so many possibilities! Check out the photos throughout this post for inspiration.

To clarify that the last stitch of the forward pass is worked differently, I always refer to this stitch in my patterns as an 'end stitch'

Carry yarn between rows if there is only a few rows between colour changes. If there are more than a few rows, then it's best to cut yarn and rejoin.

As you work, you will notice that your feather starts to lean to one side a little. That's a good thing! This will give your feather a nice natural shape

Foundation row: Using Colour A, ch 11. Starting from 2nd ch from hook, pick up a loop from the * top loop only of chain and in each ch to end (11 lps). Return

* a nicer edge is achieved for this design by working into the top loop instead of working from the usual back bump.

Row 2: M1tb, Tss 3, Tss3tog, Tss 3, M1tb, work end st (11 lps).

Return

Row 3: Work as for Row 2, changing to Colour B on the last 2 lps of return

Row 4: Continuing with Colour B, work as for Row 2, changing to Colour A on the last 2 lps of return

Row 5: Continuing with Colour A, work as for Row 2, changing to Colour B on the last 2 lps of return

Row 6: Continuing with Colour B, work as for Row 2, changing to Colour A on the last 2 lps of return

Rows 7 – 10: Continuing with Colour A, work as for Row 2

Row 11: Work as for Row 2, changing to Colour B on the last 2 lps of return

Row 12: Continuing with Colour B, work as for Row 2, changing to Colour A on the last 2 lps of return

Row 13: Continuing with Colour A, Tss 3, Tss3tog, Tss 3, work end st (9 lps). Return changing to Colour B on the last 2 lps

Row 14: Continuing with Colour B, M1tb, Tss 2, Tss3tog, Tss 2, M1tb, work end st (9 lps), changing to Colour A on the last 2 lps of return

Rows 15 – 17: Continuing with Colour A, M1tb, Tss 2, Tss3tog, Tss 2, M1tb, work end st (9 lps). Return

Row 18: Tss 2, Tss3tog, Tss 2, work end st (7 lps). Return

Row 19: M1tb, Tss 1, Tss3tog, Tss 1, M1tb, work end st (7 lps). Return

Row 20: Tss 1, Tss3tog, Tss 1, work end st (5 lps). Return

Row 21: Tss3tog, work end st (3 lps). Return: – draw yarn through all 3 lps on hook. Ch 6, sl st back down along chain. Fasten off.

Weave in ends

Small Feather:

Pattern note: The following pattern doesn't include colour change instructions.

Foundation row: Ch 9. Starting from 2nd ch from hook, pick up a loop from the * top loop only of chain and in each ch to end (9 lps). Return

Rows 2 – 10: M1tb, Tss 2, Tss3tog, Tss 2, M1tb, work end st (9 lps). Return

Row 11: Tss 2, Tss3tog, Tss 2, work end st (7 lps). Return

Rows 12 – 13: M1tb, Tss 1, Tss3tog, Tss 1, M1tb, work end st (7 lps). Return

Row 14: Tss 1, Tss3tog, Tss 1, work end st (5 lps). Return

Row 15: Tss3tog, work end st (3 lps). Return: – draw yarn through all 3 lps on hook. Ch 6, sl st back down along chain. Fasten off.

Weave in ends

Tip: You can also make your feather in a single colour and embroider your designs on later

Dreamcatcher Tutorials

Crocheted Mandala

What you need

1 ball Yarn & Colors Must-Have Minis in each color: 52 Orchid, 73 Jade Gravel, 74 Opaline Glass, 75 Green Ice, 02 Cream, 45 Blossom, 42 Peach

2 balls Yarn & Colors Must-Have Minis in 82 Grass

Crochet hook 3 mm

Metal ring 35 cm

Note:

The turning chains (tch) do not count as a stitch, they are only used to get height for the next round.

Does your work tend to get wavy? You may have too many stitches, so gradually decrease a few stitches. Otherwise, you might want to try a half-size smaller hook.

Does your work pull together too tightly? You may have too few stitches, so gradually add a few extra stitches. Otherwise, try using a half-size bigger hook.

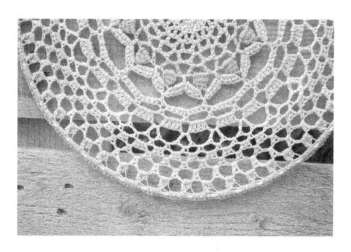

Instructions

Abbreviations used:

ch = chain

ch sp = chain space

tch = turning chain (ch sts used to get the height for the

new round)

st(s)	= stitch(es)
sl st	= slip stitch
sc	= single crochet (UK: double crochet)
hdc	= half double crochet (UK: half treble crochet)
dc	= double crochet (UK: treble crochet)
dc...tog	= double crochet ... sts together
(...)	= (work these sts in the same st)

Crochet Pattern Mandala:

Round 1: Using Orchid, work 12sc in a magic loop. Close with a sl st in the 1st sc, fasten off.

Round 2: Join Jade Gravel in any st, tch 2. Work 2dc in each st. Close with 1 sl st in the 1st dc.

Round 3: Tch 2. Continuing in the 1st st, * (1dc, ch 1, 1dc), skip 1 st. * Repeat from * to *. Close round with a sl st in the 1st dc.

Round 4: Sl st in the 1-ch sp, tch 2. Continuing in the same 1-ch sp, * (1dc, ch 2, 1dc), ch 1, continue in the next 1-ch sp. * Repeat from * to *. Close round with a sl st in the 1st dc.

Round 5: Sl st in the 2-ch sp, tch 2. Continuing in the same 2-ch sp, * (1dc, ch 3, 1dc), ch 1, continue in the next 2-ch sp. * Repeat from * to *. Close round with a sl st in the 1st dc, fasten off.

Round 6: Join Grass in any 3-ch sp, tch 2. Continuing in the same 3-ch sp, * (1dc, ch 4, 1dc), ch. 1, continue in the next 3-ch sp. * Repeat from * to *. Close round with a sl st in the 1st dc, fasten off.

Round 7: Join Orchid in any 4-ch sp, tch 2. Continuing in the same 4-ch sp, * dc7tog, ch 9, continue in the next 4-ch sp. * Repeat from * to *. Close round with a sl st in the 1st dc, fasten off.

Round 8: Join Green Ice in any 9-ch sp, tch 1. Continuing in the same 9-ch sp, * 5hdc, work 1sc in the 1-ch sp of round 6, pulling up a longer loop over round 7. 5hdc in the same 9-ch sp, then continue in the next 9-ch sp. * Repeat from * to *. Close round with a sl st in the 1st hdc.

Round 9: Tch 1. Continuing in the same 1st hdc, * 1sc, ch 9, skip group of 10 hdc. * Repeat from * to *. Close round with a sl st in the 1st sc.

Round 10: Sl st in the 9-ch sp, tch 1. 10sc in each 9-ch sp. Close round with a sl st in the 1st sc.

Round 11: Tch 1, then continue in the same sc. * 1sc, ch 5, skip 4 sts. * Repeat from * to *. Close round with a sl st in the 1st sc, fasten off.

Round 12: Join Peach in any 5-ch sp, tch 1. Continuing in the same 5-ch sp, * 1hdc, 3dc, 1hdc, ch 2, continue in the next 5-ch sp. * Repeat from * to *. Close round with a sl st in the 1st hdc, fasten off.

Round 13: Join Cream in any 2-ch sp, tch 2. Continuing in the same 2-ch sp, * 1dc, ch 3, 1dc, ch 3, continue in the next 2-ch sp. * Repeat from * to *. Close round with a sl st in the 1st dc.

Round 14: Sl st in the 3-ch sp, tch 1. Continuing in the same 3-ch sp, * 1sc, ch 3, continue in the next 3-ch sp. * Repeat from * to *. Close round with a sl st in the 1st sc, fasten off.

Round 15: Join Blossom in any 3-ch sp, tch 1. Continuing in the same 3-ch sp, * 3hdc, ch 1, continue in the next 3-ch sp. * Repeat from * to *. Close round with a sl st in the 1st hdc, fasten off.

Round 16: Join Peach in any 1-ch sp, tch 1. Continuing in the same 1-ch sp, * 2hdc, ch 2, continue in the next 1-ch sp. * Repeat from * to *. Close round with a sl st in the 1st hdc, fasten off.

Round 17: Join Cream in any 2-ch sp, tch 1. Continuing in the same 2-ch sp, * 2hdc in a 2-ch sp, ch 3. * Repeat from * to *. Close round with a sl st in the 1st hdc, fasten off.

Round 18: Join Opaline Glass in any 3-ch sp, tch 2. Continuing in the same 3-ch sp, * dc5tog, ch 3, continue in the next 3-ch sp. * Repeat from * to *. Close round with a sl st in the 1st dc, fasten off.

Round 19: Join Grass in any 3-ch sp and attach your crochet work to the metal ring by working 5sc around the metal ring in each 3-ch sp. Fasten off.

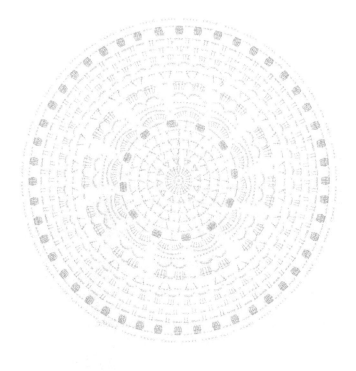

Petal Mandala

What you need

DK Yarn - Scheepjes Colour Crafter in a range of colours of your choice.

4mm hook

scissors

yarn needle

400mm steel craft hoop (you should be able to find these in a range of sizes at your local craft store. I bought mine from Spotlight in New Zealand)

Abbreviations:

sl st - slip stitch

ch - chain

sc - single crochet

dc - double crochet

tr - treble

CL - cluster

3 dc CL - 3 double crochet cluster

st(s) - stitch(es)

sp(s) - space(s)

Special Stitches:

3 dc CL - *yarn over (YO), insert hook into stitch and pull back a loop, YO and pull through 2 loops (this is a partial dc stitch)* repeat this sequence twice more, YO once more and pull though all 4 loops on hook.

Dreamcatcher Tutorials

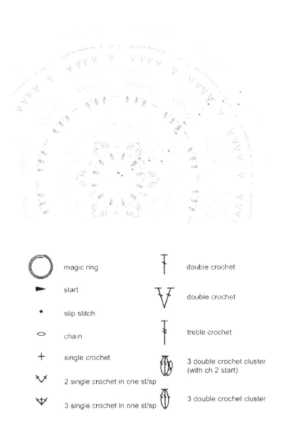

Instructions

Notes: The mandala is worked in the round. Each new round is noted with the red dot and round number on the chart.

Almost every round is started with a new colour (if you wish) so fasten off and cut ends at the end of each round, unless instructed otherwise.

Leave weaving the ends until AFTER you've crocheted the mandala to the hoop as this stretches the mandala and can cause the ends to unravel or restrict the work from stretching evenly.

The outer rounds of this mandala can ruffle slightly, which disappears when the mandala is stretched onto the hoop.

Your finished mandala will be significantly smaller than the hoop. This is necessary and allows the mandala to sit taut within the hoop. If you wish to crop the mandala (or add further rounds) you will need to ensure that you have a decent space between the mandala (laid flat) and the ring (the size of this space changes depending on the size of the hoop). To test if the space is adequate, use stitch markers or scrap yarn to temporarily attach your mandala to the hoop at even intervals around the circumference - if your mandala is saggy, remove a round or two, and if you have to pull too hard to get it to fit, add an extra round or two).

* For the rainbow coloured mandala I added extra chain rounds after R12 continuing in the same fashion - e.g. R 12 is "ch 3, sc..." so an extension of this for the next row becomes "ch 4, sc..." and "ch 5, sc" for the following round until you reach the desired diameter.

Round 1:

Magic ring, ch 3 (counts as the first dc), 11 dc into the ring, join with a sl st to the first dc (3rd ch st), pull the tail to close

(12).

Round 2:

Join with a sl st in one of the dc sts, ch 2 (counts as first partial dc in 3 dc cluster) and complete cluster in the same st, *ch 1, 3 dc CL in the next st* repeat this sequence to the end of the round, join with a sl st to the top of the first CL.

(24)

Round 3:

Join with a sl st in any ch 1 space. *{sl st, ch 2, dc, tr, ch 2, tr, dc, ch 2, sl st} in the ch 1 sp, skip CL, 2 sc in next ch 1 sp, skip CL* repeat this sequence to the end of the round, join with a sl st in the first sl st.

(6 'petals' & 12 sc)

Round 4:

Join with a sl st in the second of any of the 2 sc groups, ch 5 (counts as the first dc & ch 2), dc in the same st, *ch 1, skip {sl st, ch 2, dc, tr}, 2 sc in the ch 2 sp, ch 1, skip {tr, dc, 2 ch, sl st, sc}, [dc, ch 2, dc: v-st] in the next sc st* repeat this sequence to the end of the row, join with a sl st to the top of the first dc (3rd ch st). DO NOT CUT YARN (unless you want to change colours for the next round).

(6 v-st, 12 sc, 6 ch 1)

Round 5:

ch 1 (does not count), sc in the same st, 3 sc in ch 2 sp, sc the next st, sc in the ch 1 sp, sc in the next sc st, 2 sc in the next st, sc in the ch 1 sp, *sc in the next dc, 3 sc in the ch 2 sp, sc in the next dc, sc in the ch 1 sp, sc in the next st, 2 sc in the next sc, sc in the ch 1 sp* repeat this sequence to the end of the round, join with a sl st to the first sc.

(60 sc)

Round 6:

Join with a sl st in the middle st of one of the 3 sc groups, ch 3 (count as a dc), 2 dc in the same sp, ch 6, skip 4 sts, *3 dc in the next st, ch 6, skip 4 sts* repeat this sequence to the end of the round, join with a sl st to the first dc st (3rd ch st).

(12 x 3dc, 12 x ch 6)

Round 7:

Join with a sl st in one of the ch 6 spaces, ch 2 (counts as first partial dc in 3 dc cluster) and complete cluster in the same st, {ch 1, 3 dc CL, ch 1, 3 dc CL} in the same sp, ch 3, skip 3 dc, *{3 dc CL, ch 1, 3 dc CL, ch 1, 3 dc CL} in the next ch 6 sp, ch 3, skip 3 dc* repeat this sequence to the end of the round, join with a sl st to the top of the first CL.

(12 x {3 dc CL/ch 1/ 3dc CL/ch1 / 3dc CL} groups, 12 x ch 3)

Round 8:

Join with a sl st in the first ch 1 sp of one of the cluster groups, ch 5 (count as tr ch 1), {tr, ch 1, tr} in the same sp, skip CL, {tr, ch 1, tr, ch 1, tr} in the next ch 1 sp, skip ch 3, *{tr, ch 1, tr, ch 1, tr} in the next ch 1 sp, skip CL, repeat {..}, skip ch 3* repeat this sequence to the end of the round, join with a sl st to the top of the first tr (4th ch st).

(72 tr, 48 ch)

Round 9:

The stitches in this round are worked into the ch 1 spaces and the gap between the central 2 tr stitches in each tr/ch1 group). The tr stitches are ignored/skipped in this round.

Join with a sl st in the first ch 1 in one of the tr/ch 1... groups, ch 2 (counts as first partial dc in 3 dc cluster) and complete cluster in the same sp, ch 1, 3 dc CL in the next ch 1 sp, ch 1, 3 dc CL in the gap between the next 2 tr sts, ch 1, {3 dc CL, ch 1} in each of the next 2 ch 1 sps, *{3 dc CL, ch 1} in the next 2 ch 1 sps, 3 dc CL in the gap between the next 2 tr sts, ch 1, {3 dc CL, ch 1} in each of the next 2 ch 1 sps* repeat this sequence for each of the {tr/ch 1, tr...} groups, join with a sl st to the top of the first CL.

(60 x 3 dc CL, 48 ch)

Round 10:

The stitches in this round are worked into the ch 1 spaces and the gap between the last CL of a group and the first CL of the next group. The CL stitches are ignored/skipped in this round.

Join with a sl st in the first ch 1 sp of one of the {CL, ch 1...} groups, ch 3 (count as dc), dc in the same sp, 2 dc in each of the next 3 ch 1 sps, *2 dc in the gap between the last CL and the first CL of the next group, 2 dc in each of the next 4 ch 1 sps8 repeat this sequence to the end of the round, join with a sl st to the first dc (3rd ch).

(120 dc)

Round 11:

The stitches in this round are worked in the spaces between the 2 dc groups. The tops of the dc stitches are ignored.

Join with a sc in one of the gaps between two 2 dc groups, ch 2, skip the tops of the next 2 dc sts, sc in the gap before the next 2 dc group, ch 2* repeat this sequence to the end of the round, join with a sl st to the first sc.

(60 sc, 60 ch 2)

Round 12:

Join with a sc in one of the ch 2 sps, ch 3, skip sc, *sc in the next ch 2 sp, ch 3, skip sc* repeat this sequence to the end of the round, join with a sl st to the first sc.

(60 sc, 60 ch 3)

Round 13:

This round joins the mandala to the hoop. The stitches are worked as you normally would, except you hold the mandala in line with, and in front of the steel hoop. Insert your hook into the stitch, AROUND the inside edge of the hoop from the front to the back. The working yarn is held at the top edge of the hoop and is picked up by the hook at the back edge. The sc stitch is completed as you normally would, giving a little tug to keep the stitch tight before beginning the next sc stitch.

Join with a sc in one of the ch 3 sps, 5 sc in the same sp, skip sc, *6 dc in the next ch 3 sp, skip sc* repeat this sequence to the end of the round, join with a sl st to the first sc st.

(360 sc)

Now is the time to weave in the ends and create a plaited rope to hang the mandala to the tree. To make the rope, gather 3 colours of yarn (from your mandala) and cut 2 x lengths approx. 1m long from each colour. Hold the strands together evenly and fold them in half. Poke the folded end into a gap in the last round of your mandala and thread the tails back through the loop, around the hoop, and pull tight (or simply tie them on if it is easier). Proceed to plait the rope, finish with a knot and trim the ends.

Spiral Dream Catcher

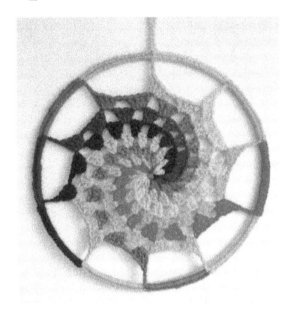

What you need

Very Small amounts of coloured yarn. I have used Stylecraft Special Dk. You can use as many colours as you like but I recommend no more than 6 or 7 while you practise the technique.

You will also need a 4.0mm hook but it is not crictical and one stitch holder for each colour .

Finally you will need a ring to hang it all in. The ones I have used are about 25 cm in diameter but again it is not critical and the pattern will explain how to adjust the size of the crochet to fit the ring. You can buy dream catcher rings from ebay or you can use embroidery hoops but I have also removed the rings from old lamp shades because I love recycling.

Instructions

You don't need to read the red bits unless you want to add more colours or adjust the size.

1. 7ch. Join into a ring with a ss. This is suitable for 7 colours.

TIP: If you can do a magic circle instead of the 7 ch it is much easier to add more colours to the pattern. If not then you should increase the length of the starting chain by 1ch for every 2 colours you add.

2. 2ch, 1tr into the ring, 1ch insert stitch holder.

TIP: If you know how to crochet over the short ends it will save hiding them later,

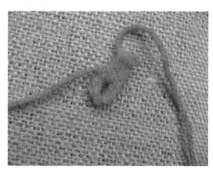

3. Join the next colour to the ring and repeat 2 above.

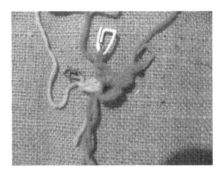

4. Repeat until you have used up all your colours.

TIP: The piece looks like a unicorn nest by now and it is a really good idea to run in the short ends at this point. If you haven't done so already.

5. Pick a colour, remove the stitch marker and make 2tr, in the gap between the 2ch and the tr of the next colour then 1ch before inserting the stitch marker..So above the dark yarn has been crocheted into the red, the red in the orange etc.

Repeat this with each colour until you get back to where you started.

6. The next round is crocheted into the 1ch space just after the first treble. The hook in the picture above is showing where the orange yarn will make the next pair of trebles. So as before pick a colour, 2tr in the 1ch space of the next colour and then 1ch. Repeat for each colour.

7. Pick a colour 2tr in the next 1ch space of the following colour then 2ch, repeat all round.

8. 2tr in each 2ch space, and then 2ch. all round changing colours as before.

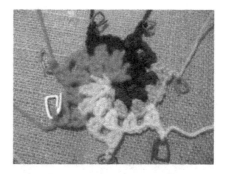

9. Repeat number 8

TIP: You may find that your crochet spiral is becoming a bit dome shaped but it does not matter as you will be stretching it onto the hoop later.

10. This time work 3 trebles into the 2ch space of the following colour then 3ch, repeat all round.

11. 3tr in the 3ch space of the following colour, 3ch repeat all round.

12. 4tr in the 3ch space of the following colour , 3ch repeat all round.

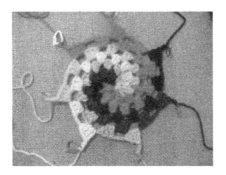

13 Repeat round 12

14. 5tr in three ch space of the following colour 2ch repeat all round.

Joining the crochet and the hoop

If you are following the pattern and not making a change in number of colours or size of hoop, then you will need roughly 230 dc to cover the entire ring. Since I have used 7 colours I will need 230 divided by 7 or approximately 33 stitches in each colour.

1. Put the yarn over the top of the hoop and the hook underneath. Pick up the yarn and pull it through the stitch on the hook. Now

work 33 dc around the hoop. This feels a bit awkward to start with but if you imagine that the hoop is like the ring at the start of the project it might be easier.

2. Cut the yarn leaving about 4cm. Remove the hook from the work and pick up the next colour before putting the hook back in the dropped loop. Yarn over, through both loops on the hook. Make 33 dc around the hoop covering the 4cm tail at the same time if you can.

3. Repeat number 2 above for each colour in turn then join the last colour to the first using a ss.

4. Make 25 chain to form the hanging loop.

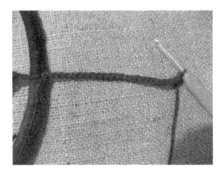

5. ss into the base of the chain, cut the yarn and hide the end.

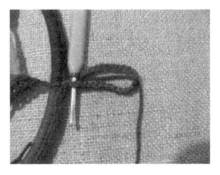

Dreamcatcher With Mille Colori

What you need

- 1 ball Mille Colori Socks & Lace Luxe colour 53

- 1 ball Yarn and Colors Must-Have Minis colour 34

- Metal ring Ø 45cm

- Crochet hook 4mm

- Leftovers of ribbon or scraps of yarn in different colours

Special stitch:

Popcorn stitch: Dc. 5, remove your hook from the loop, insert it in the loop of the first dc. Put the other loop back on your hook and draw through the first loop.

Tip: To make sure your dreamcatcher remains round you need to increase stitches in a different place each round. Increase 6 popcorn stitches each round.

Tip: When your work tends to get lumpy then stop the increases and work one round without increasing. Then in the next round start increasing again. When your work still is lumpy then work another round without increasing.

Instructions

Start with a magic ring.

Round 1: Ch. 2, popcorn 1, ch. 3, repeat from *to* 5x. Close with sl.st. 1 in the first st. (6 popcorns)

Round 2: Sl.st. 1 in the 3-ch. space, ch. 2 *popcorn 1, ch. 3, popcorn 1, ch. 3 in the same ch. space, go to the next ch. space.* Repeat from *to* 5x. Close with a sl.st. 1 in the first st. (12 popcorns)

Round 3: Sl.st. 1 in the 3-ch. space, ch. 2, *Popcorn 1, ch. 3, go to the next ch. space, popcorn 1, ch. 3. popcorn 1, ch. 3 in the same ch. space, go to the next ch. space* Repeat from *to* 5x. Close with sl.st. 1 in the first st. (18 popcorns)

Round 4: Sl.st. 1 in the 3-ch. space, ch. 2 **Popcorn 1, ch. 3, popcorn 1, ch. 3 in the same ch. space, go to the next ch. space , popcorn 1, ch. 3, go to the next ch. space popcorn 1, ch. 3, go to the next ch. space* Repeat from *to* 5x. Close with sl.st. 1 in the first st. (24 popcorns)

Round 5: Sl.st. 1 in the 3-ch. space, ch. 2 *Popcorn 1, ch. 3, popcorn 1, ch. 3 in the same ch. space, go to the next ch. space, popcorn 1, ch. 3, go to the next ch. space, popcorn 1, ch. 3, go to the next ch. space, popcorn 1, ch. 3, go to the next ch. space* Repeat from *to* 5x. Close with sl.st. 1 in the first st. (6 times increasing = 30 popcorns)

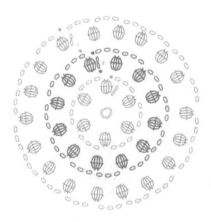

Continue this way. Increase in the rows as is described below. Divide the increases such that your work remains nicely round.

Round 6: (36 popcorns) 6 increases

Round 7: (42 popcorns) 6 increases

Round 8: (48 popcorns) 6 increases

Round 9: (55 popcorns) 7 increases

Round 10: (61 popcorns) 6 increases

Round 11: (68 popcorns) 7 increases

Round 12: (68 popcorns) no increases

Round 13: (68 popcorns) no increases

Round 14: (68 popcorns) no increases

Round 15: (68 popcorns) no increases

Round 16: (75 popcorns) 7 increases

Round 17: (75 popcorns)

Finishing:

Work 17 rounds and join your dreamcatcher with sc. to the metal ring using Yarn and Colors Must-have Minis colour 34.

Decorate your dreamcatcher with cheerful coloured ribbons or yarns.

Brown Spiral Dream Catcher

Stitches/abbreviations used:

ch - chain

sl st - slip stitch (UK - single crochet)

sc - single crochet (UK - double crochet)

dc - double crochet (UK - treble)

tr - treble (double treble)

puff stitch - dc 5 sts worked together in same stitch

dc3tog (dc decrease) - dc worked together in 3 consecutive stitches

Dreamcatcher Tutorials

Instruction:

Using colour A, ch 6, join the last ch to the first ch with a sl st to form a ring.

Round 1: Ch 5 (counts as 1st tr + ch 1), **treble into the ring, ch 1** Repeat from ** to ** 14 more times. Join with a sl st to the 4th ch (16 sts). Fasten off colour A.

Round 2: Join colour B and ch 3 (counts as 1st dc), 2 dc in next ch-1 space, ** dc in next tr, 2 dc in next space** Repeat from ** to ** around. Join with a sl st to the 3rd ch (48 sts). Fasten off yarn.

Round 3: Join colour C and ch 6, dc in same st, **skip 2 dc, (dc, ch 3, dc) in next dc** Repeat from ** to ** around. Join with a sl st to 3rd ch. Fasten off yarn.

Round 4: Join colour D in next ch-3 space, **puff stitch in ch-3 space, ch 4** Repeat from ** to ** around. Join to the top of 1st puff stitch.

Round 5: Ch 3, **5 dc in next ch-4 space, dc in next puff stitch** Repeat from ** to ** around. Join with a sl st to the 3rd ch (96 sts). Fasten off yarn.

Round 6: Join colour E, ch 2, dc2tog (counts as 1st dc3tog), ch 3, **dc3tog, ch 3** Repeat from ** to ** around. Join with a sl st to the 1st dc3tog. Fasten off yarn.

Round 7: Join colour F in next ch-3 space, ch 1 and sc in same space, **ch 5, sc in next ch-3 space** Repeat from ** to ** around but instead of the last ch-5 make ch 2 and dc in the sc at the beginning of round.

Round 8: Ch 1, sc in same space, **ch 6, sc in next ch-5 space**

Repeat from ** to ** around and instead of the last ch-6 make ch 3 and dc in the sc at the beginning of round.

Round 9: Ch 1, sc in same space, **ch 7, sc in next ch-6 space** Repeat from ** to ** around and instead of the last ch-7 make ch 4 and dc in the sc at the beginning of round.

Round 10: Join colour G in the same st, ch 1 and sc in same st, **9 dc in next ch-7 space, sc in next ch-7 space** Repeat from ** to ** around. Fasten off yarn and weave in all the loose ends.

Your mandala is now ready and if you are going to make the dreamcatcher get your hoop ready. Wrapping yarn around the hoop was the most annoying part for me. Sew the middle stitch of each shell to the hoop. Then tie all your decorative items to the bottom of the hoop. Also make a loop at the top for hanging your dreamcatcher.

Printed in the USA
CPSIA information can be obtained
at www.ICGtesting.com
LVHW092328070224
771285LV00031B/836